COOKING

à la Française

Family Recipes with and without Pressure Cooker

WILDSIDE PRESS

FOREWORD

The modern hostess might be caricatured as a Janus like creature with one face toward the drawing room, the other toward the kitchen. She must be able with grace to leap from the foyer into the fire, to entertain her guests charmingly and linger with deceiving insouciance over her cocktail, and at the right moment to retire unobtrusively and produce as if by magic a delectable dinner.

As every woman knows, not magic but hard work and master strategy lie behind this achievement. The hostess must have prepared her menu thoughtfully with consideration not only for the excellence of her food but also for the apparent ease with which it can be produced and served. In America there is too much reliance on the short order type of meal, the frozen vegetables, the packaged ingredients.

The collection of recipes in this book is designed to solve some of the culinary problems of the hostess who would like to rely less on the cocktails and more on the food to stimulate and delight her guests. They have been chosen by one, who being French and brought up in France, has long been familiar with the merits of French cooking.

The special taste and flavor of French cuisine is due for a great part to the generous use of such herbs as parsley, tarragon, shallots, onions, garlic, etc. It is therefore quite important to find a market where they can always be obtained. Most Italian markets carry them.

Timid souls must not be frightened by the large amounts of garlic used in certain recipes. The fact, and it is not a well known one, is that, although raw garlic has a very potent taste and odor, cooked garlic is unrecognizable in a dish.

These recipes provide no short-cut to the delectable cooking of French kitchens, they require resourceful buying of foods and condiments and they presuppose a willingness on the part of the cook to spend much time and patience in the early stages of preparing the food. They also demand the standard equipment of French cooks, earthenware casseroles of various sizes and shape and a Dutch oven. A great assortment of sturdy earthenware pots and pans is to be found at the Bazar Français in New York City at 666, 6th Avenue.

The flavor and taste of certain French dishes derives often from their slow cooking in a tightly closed casserole. Through this process the various ingredients are subtley blended together. However, by means of a pressure cooker, the same blending together of the various flavors can usually be achieved in 12 to 20 minutes instead of several hours.

For the cook who is willing to take thought for the morrow and eager to escape from the banality of too familiar menus, "Cooking á la Française" should prove an exciting culinary adventure and a happy introduction to French cooking without tears.

CONTENTS

SOUPS

I   Onion Soup.

Peel a few onions and cut in thin slices. Sauté in butter
until they become golden brown. Sprinkle with a tablespoonful
of flour. Add consommé or hot water and simmer one-half
hour. Season with salt and pepper and pour into individual casserole dishes. Place on each casserole a slice or two of dry
buttered bread covered with grated Parmesan cheese and brown
in oven.

II   Leek and Potato Soup.

Cut white parts of leeks and potatoes into small pieces and
cook in salted boiling water. When soft mash vegetables into
the liquid part through food mill. Add some milk. Reheat.
Taste for seasoning. Put one teaspoon butter into each individual serving dish and pour in liquid.

Soupe aux poireaux
or pommes de terre

III   Water-Cress Soup.

Same as above substituting water - cress for leeks.

IV   <u>Cauliflower Soup.</u>

     1 cauliflower.
     1-1/2 quart of consommé.
     1 cup milk.
     1 stick of butter.
     4 egg yolks.
     Salt.

    Separate cauliflower into small flowerettes and cook in boiling slightly salted water until soft. Mash through strainer or food mill and add consommé. Place over a slow fire and let simmer fifteen minutes. Remove from fire and add milk and butter. Taste for seasoning. Dilute egg yolks in one or two spoonfuls of water then add to mixture. Return to low heat and stir until mixture is thick enough to coat the spoon. Do not allow to boil after you have mixed in the egg yolks.

soupe à l'oignon

V   <u>Baked Onion Soup.</u>

(Can be used as a luncheon dish.)

     Stale \bread. Fresh butter.
     Onions, Swiss cheese.
     Tomato paste, salt.

Brown bread in oven and cover each piece with a generous coating of butter and cheese. (Butter first.) Slice the onions, one for each helping and sauté in butter until they are a nice golden brown. In an earthenware deep dish place the slices of bread in alternating layers with the onions. Begin with layer of bread; end with layer of onions. When you have arranged half of your slices of bread you cover this layer with tomato paste using three quarters of a tablespoonful for each person. Continue the layers and on the last one place more tomato paste. This time half a tablespoonful per person. Cover the top with a thick layer of grated cheese. Don't fill the dish more than three quarters full. Placing a funnel or a tube that reaches to the bottom of the dish you will slowly pour into it some hot water that has been slightly salted. The mass will rise an inch or two and float. Place the dish uncovered on a low flame and cook for thirty minutes. Then if the mixture has become too dry add some more boiling water always using the tube or funnel.

Then place the dish in a very low oven for one hour. When the dish is done the crust on top is crisp and golden and the inside forms a pureé in which it is impossible to distinguish the various ingredients.

VI   Soupe du Père Tranquille.

(So-called because it is supposed to induce a good night's sleep.)

For four persons take two heads of romaine and one can of consommé to which an equal amount of water has been added.

Quarter the heads of romaine and throw them into the boiling consommé. Use only a small quantity of the consommé and cook slowly until the mixture forms a puree. Then add the rest of the consommé.

Put some slices of stale bread and a tablespoonful of butter at the bottom of a soup turreen. Pour the soup into the turreen, cover for two or three minutes and serve.

VII   Potage Velouté. (Velvet Soup)

Consommé - 2 quarts.
Egg yolks - 4.
Cream of rice - 10 tablespoonfuls.

Mix the cream of rice with one cup of cold consommé working it so as to get a very smooth mixture. Place the rest of the
consommé over the flame in a saucepan. When it boils pour into it the cream of rice mixture stirring with wire whisk. Leave
pan uncovered and allow to simmer for fifteen minutes.
Remove from fire. Allow to cool for three or four minutes
then add the egg yolks mixed with a small quantity of cold
consommé. Place over fire again until it thickens slightly
stirring all the time and not allowing the mixture to boil.
Before serving add a few leaves of tarragon if you have them.

VIII   Split Pea Soup. (for 6)

2 cups split peas.
1-1/2 quarts water. One cup milk.
Medium size onion. Cloves.
Butter the size of an egg (or bacon fat).
One small bunch of parsley with celery
leaves.

A ham bone if available is a very excellent addition.

Soak peas in water over night. Cook in cold water with
onion, parsley and celery. Let simmer two or three hours
or until tender. Mash the peas and add the milk and more
water if necessary. Taste for seasoning. Serve with
crôutons fried in butter.

This dish could be done in much less time in a pressure
cooker - fifteen minutes with pointer at Cook. Let pointer
return to off position.
If less water is used a thicker pureé is obtained which
makes, with link sausages, a very substantial pièce de résistance for a luncheon.

SAUCES

I   Sauce Béchamel.

     1-1/2 cups of stock.
     1 cup scalded milk.
     1/4 cup butter.   1/4 cup flour.
     1/2 teaspoon salt.
     1/8 teaspoon pepper.

Melt butter in saucepan over a very slow fire or in a double boiler. Add flour and gradually hot stock and milk. Add, if desired, one slightly beaten egg yolk diluted with small quantity of hot sauce. Salt and pepper.

If no stock is available milk only can be used.

II   Sauce Mornay.

Béchamel sauce into which some grated Gruyère cheese is incorporated together with some mushroom juice if available.

III   Sauce Hollandaise.

For eight people take a stick of butter, three egg yolks, the juice of a lemon, salt and pepper.

In a double boiler place the egg yolks, lemon juice, salt and pepper and one third of the stick of butter. Stir constantly with wire whisk until butter melts. Add second piece of butter, and, as mixture thickens, third piece. Remove from fire and season. If mixture curdles add two tablespoons heavy cream or boiling water, drop by drop.

IV   Sauce Béarnaise.

In a saucepan put a cup of good wine vinegar, three shallotts and one clove of garlic. Let it simmer for about one hour and a half or until the liquid is half evaporated.

In a double boiler place three egg yolks, salt and pepper and the vinegar with the shallotts and garlic mashed into a pulp. Add to it a stick of butter doing it gradually, one small piece at a time, some tarragon leaves and parsley cut up fine.

A Béarnaise sauce is really a Hollandaise sauce flavored with vinegar, shallotts and garlic.

V   Sauce Mousseline.

A Hollandaise sauce into which has been incorporated a teaspoon of cornstarch and a small quantity of whipped cream. Whip up the Sauce Mousseline before serving.

VI   Sauce Tomate.

Cut the tomatoes and onions into small pieces and cook in a pan with shallotts and parsley and a bay leaf. In another pan put a tablespoonful of butter and when it is melted stir in a tablespoonful of flour. When it begins to brown add a cup of warm consommé or water. Strain the tomato mixture and add it to the second pan. Let it simmer over a slow fire for about an hour stirring from time to time.

This sauce can be made much more quickly by using, instead of the raw tomatoes, four tablespoonfuls of Italian tomato paste The cooking time is then reduced to three minutes.

VII   Sauce <u>Madère</u>

Take a tablespoonful of butter or bacon fat - melt it in a
saucepan with about half a dozen cubes of fat back. Stir in a
heaping tablespoonful of flour, one onion chopped up, one carrot
chopped up, a sprig of thyme, parsley, one bay leaf. Then add a
pint of stock or water and a spoonful of tomato paste. Cook for
at least an hour or until the sauce is very much reduced, by
about half, and thicker. Strain the sauce and add half a cup of
Madeira wine. Do not boil the sauce after the wine has been
added.

VIII   Sauce <u>Soubise</u>.

1/2 lb. onions.
1 tablespoonful butter.
1 tablespoonful flour.
1 cup stock or milk.
2 tablespoonfuls double cream.

Parboil the onions 7 or 8 minutes. Then mince them and
place them in a saucepan with a good teaspoonful of butter.
Cover the saucepan and cook for about 15 or 20 minutes. Then
sprinkle the flour over the onions, add the stock or milk and stir
until the mixture reaches the boiling point. Season with salt
and pepper; cóver the pan and cook over a low flame for almost
an hour stirring from time to time. Mash through strainer or
food mill. If the puree is too thick add a few spoonfuls of stock
or milk. Taste for seasoning; reheat. At the last moment add
the remaining butter and the cream.

This sauce usually accompanies a pork roast.

To Marinate.

I   3 cups white wine - 1 cup vinegar.
3 shallots - 1 clove garlic.
3 onions (sliced) - pepper.
Parsley, tarragon, thyme, bay leaf.

II   Same as above with one cup olive oil added.

RICE DISHES

I   <u>Spanish Rice</u>.

1 cup rice.
3 cups consommé or water.
1 tablespoonful butter.
1 onion.
1 spoonful tomato paste.
Salt, pepper, nutmeg to taste.
Left over meat (chicken, veal, pork,
crab meat, lobster meat)

If canned crab or lobster meat is used their liquor should be used instead of consommé or water to cook the rice. If consommé is used instead of water very little salt is needed.

Brown the finely minced onion in butter. Add the rice and fry it well, stirring occasionally. Cover with consommé or water, add the tomato paste and other ingredients. Turn into a buttered baking dish and bake in a moderate oven for about 45 minutes or until rice is soft and fluffy.

In France this dish is always made with mussels, a delicious shell fish, and the water of the mussels, which is salted is used to cook the rice.

Riz à l'espagnole

II   Rice with Mushrooms. (4 to 6 portions)

2-1/2 cups sliced fresh mushrooms.
1/3 cup olive oil.
2/3 cup rice.
2 large onions, minced.
1/2 clove garlic, minced.
3 tablespoons tomato pureé.
2 tablespoons minced parsley.
1/2 teaspoon salt.

Sauté mushrooms in hot olive oil until golden brown. Remove mushrooms from oil and replace with onion, garlic and then the rice. Cook stirring occasionally until rice browns. Turn into buttered baking dish. Add tomato pureé, parsley, salt, mushrooms, mixing lightly. Cover with water, or consommé or stock to 1/2 inch above rice. Cover and bake in a moderate oven about 45 minutes or until rice is soft and fluffy.

III   Risotto. (Italian Style)

The rice is prepared as in the preceding recipes but instead of meat or fish, cheese is added. 3/4 cup Parmesan or Gruyère cheese is mixed with the rice before baking and some cheese and butter sprinkled on top.

MACARONI

I   Italian Macaroni· (for 6)

1/2 lb· macaroni·
1/2 cup grated Gruyère·
1/2 cup grated Parmesan·
1 tablespoonful butter· (heaping)

Throw the macaroni into 1-1/2 quart of boiling salted water·
Simmer for about 12 or 15 minutes· Drain in colander then
put back in saucepan over fire for a few minutes to dry· Add
butter and cheese· Toss together lightly with fork and spoon until cheese melts but be careful not to cook cheese· Serve on
hot platter·

II   Macaroni fourré·

Boil macaroni as in the preceding recipe· Then in a buttered baking dish arrange alternate layers of macaroni and left
over meat cut in small pieces· Add one cup of consommé, one
tablespoonful of tomato pureé and top the last layer with a good
sprinkling of grated cheese and melted butter· Brown in oven·

III   Macaroni au gratin·

Boil macaroni· Make 2-1/2 cups of Béchamel sauce· Add
1/2 cup of grated cheese to the sauce· Place macaroni in a buttered baking dish and pour Béchamel over it· Sprinkle on top
a good layer of grated cheese and melted butter and bake in slow
oven·

IV   Spaghetti·

For eight or ten people cook one pound of spaghetti in salted
boiling water· Arrange spaghetti in deep soup plates and serve
with the following sauce:

6 or 7 onions.
2 green peppers.
1 lb. chuck steak (ground)
2 cans tomato paste
1 can tomatoes.
1 pod red pepper, seeded.

Slice the onions and green peppers very fine and sauté with the meat in olive oil. When the meat is done add the tomato paste, can of tomatoes, red pepper, salt, cover and allow to simmer for five or six hours. Serve with freshly grated Parmesan cheese.

V   Gnocchi. (Serves 4)

3 cups milk.
3/4 cup hominy grits.
3/4 teaspoon salt.
2 egg yolks.
1 cup light white sauce.
3 tablespoonfuls butter.
3/4 cup Parmesan cheese.

Make a mush of 3 cups milk and 3/4 cup of hominy grits. Bring milk to a boil. Sprinkle in grits gradually, stirring constantly. Cook and stir until mixture thickens and begins to spit. Place covered over hot water and cook for thirty minutes. Remove and immediately beat in two tablespoonfuls butter and two egg yolks. Spread on buttered dish so mixture is about half an inch thick. Chill - Cut in small squares. Arrange in buttered baking dish a layer of mush squares, sprinkle liberally with parmesan cheese; dot with butter. Repeat.

Pour over one cup light white sauce: (one tablespoon butter, one tablespoon flour, one cup milk, salt, pepper.) Top with cheese and bake half an hour at 350° or until top is well browned.

EGGS

Omelet

In order to be successful when making an omelet it is necessary to use a heavy iron skillet and to make sure that it is very smooth. If it is not, put it over the fire with a dot of butter and a handful of salt. Rub vigorously and your pan is then ready. Do not try to make too large an omelet: 10 eggs should be the maximum - otherwise the omelet will be too large and heavy to handle and shape in the pan.

The basic recipe is as follows:

> 5 eggs.
> 4 tablespoons cream or milk.
> 3/4 teaspoon salt. 1/8 teaspoon pepper.
> 2 heaping tablespoons butter.

While the butter is melting in the pan beat up the eggs and cream and seasoning vigorously. While melting the butter 'sings.' When it stops is the moment to pour the eggs into the pan. Reduce heat slightly. As the omelet cooks, lift with spatula, letting uncooked part run underneath. Omelet should be rather creamy inside. Fold and turn on hot platter.

There are many variations of this basic recipe.

omelette fine herbe

I   Omelet <u>fines</u> <u>herbes</u>.

Cut up very fine into the eggs a handful of parsley, chives and tarragon leaves before pouring them into the pan.

II   <u>Mushroom Omelet</u>.

Slice one or two handfuls of mushrooms and sauté them in butter. When they are almost done add a few sprigs of parsley cut up very fine and before pouring the eggs over the mushrooms add some more butter in the pan.

omelette aux champignons.

III   <u>Potatoes Omelet</u>.

Boil one or two potatoes according to the size of your omelet and when they are almost done peel and slice them. Brown them in butter with a few sprigs of parsley and a small clove of garlic cut up very fine..

Before pouring the eggs over the potatoes add some more butter in the pan.

IV   <u>Cheese Omelet</u>.

Proceed with the basic recipe and fold into your omelet the desired amount of grated Gruyère or Parmesan cheese.

V   <u>Spanish Omelet</u>.

When the omelet is ready on the serving platter cover it with a tomato sauce that has been kept heated and ready.

Egg Dishes.

I   Eggs Mornay.

Place a poached egg in a buttered individual mold or ramikin, cover with Sauce Mornay and put in the oven for a few minutes.

II   Eggs in Jelly.

Place a cold poached egg in an individual ramikin. Fill the ramikin with consommé Madrilène and chill in refrigerator.

III   Fondue.

Put in a saucepan a spoonful of butter and when it is melted sprinkle over it a spoonful of flour. Add 2 egg yolks well beaten and half a cup of milk. Let the mixture boil for about two minutes stirring all the time with a wooden spoon. Take the saucepan off the fire and add a cupful of grated Gruyère cheese and the 2 egg whites beaten stiff. Pour mixture into individual buttered ramikins or a baking dish and cook in slow oven. Do not fill the dishes more than three quarters full as the mixture rises.

IV   ‑Quiche Lorraine·

Line a 9 inch pie plate with pie crust dough· Cut twelve
thin slices of ham and the same number of slices of Swiss or
Gruyère cheese· Arrange them in layers over the pie crust
dough· Beat together four eggs, one tablespoon flour, a gene‑
rous grating of nutmeg, half a teaspoon salt and a few grains of
cayenne· Add two cups of thin cream and last, stir in one and
a half tablespoonfuls melted sweet butter· Strain this custard
over the ham and cheese· Bake in a moderate oven for about
40 minutes or until the custard is set and nicely browned·

Serve hot or cold· Served cold with beer it makes an excel‑
lent dish for a buffet supper·

V   Ham Soufflé·

3 heaping tablespoons butter· 4 eggs·
3 tablespoons flour· 1 cup scalded milk.
3/4 teaspoon salt·

Left over ham, at least 1/4 lb·, ground fine and marinated in
a wine glass of brandy·

Melt butter, add flour and, gradually, scalded milk· Bring
to boiling point and pour onto egg yolks beaten until lemon color‑
ed· Add salt and pepper, the egg whites beaten stiff and last the
ham and brandy·

Set in a pan of hot water and bake in a moderate oven from
30 to 40 minutes·

VI   Cheese Soufflé·

Proceed in the same manner as for the Ham Soufflé substitut‑
ing 1/2 cup of grated cheese for the ham· Omit brandy·

FISH

Sea-Bass Niçoise.

4 sea-bass, 3/4 lb each.
6 tomatoes.
1 big onion minced.
1 clove garlic minced.
1 bay leaf.
Butter, bacon fat, or olive oil, salt and pepper.

Peel and quarter the tomatoes. Press slightly to get rid of the water and seeds. Heat the fat in a large but shallow baking dish. Sauté the tomatoes, onions and garlic. Dip the fish in milk seasoned with salt and pepper, then in flour.

Place the fish in the baking dish and bake about 45 minutes uncovered.

II   Cod Fish Home Style.

1-1/2 lbs. cod-fish.
2 lbs. boiled potatoes.
18 cloves garlic.
1 cup olive oil.
Ground pepper - parsley.

Soak fish overnight in lukewarm water. To cook, cover with fresh water and bring to a boil. Let simmer very gently for about ten minutes. Drain and flake fish, removing skin and bones. Cut boiled potatoes and garlic into thin slices. Heat oil in a shallow casserole. Add garlic and cook until it becomes transparent. Then add the potatoes and flaked fish. Season to taste. Sprinkle with chopped parsley. Reheat and serve in casserole in which it was cooked.

Brandade de Morue
ou Morue à la Provencale

III   Brandade de Morue (Cod Fish).

1 lb. dry salt cod.
1/2 cup olive oil.
1/2 cup milk.
1 clove garlic.
Juice of one lemon.
Pinch of nutmeg, white pepper.

Prepare cod fish as in previous recipe. Add garlic and put it through a meat grinder. Place the fish in a saucepan over a very low fire and stir the hot olive oil into it with a wooden spoon, one drop at a time. Stir in the warm milk in the same manner. The brandade must present the appearance of a smooth and thick white pureé. Season with pepper, nutmeg, the juice of one lemon and salt, if necessary.

IV   Cod Fish en Timbale.

Prepare cod fish as in previous recipe. Add Bechamel, Mornay, or Soubise sauce, allowing one cup of sauce to each pound of fish. Turn into a buttered baking dish. Sprinkle with grated cheese, if desired. Brown in oven.

V   Cod fish Provencale.

Heat 4 or 5 tablespoons of olive oil in a Dutch oven or a large and deep casserole. Cut up fine one large onion, one clove garlic, one leek, three tomatoes. Brown in the hot olive oil. Add 1 pint of water, pepper, thyme, bay leaf. Simmer for 15 minutes. Add quartered potatoes. Cook until potatoes are done. Add the cod fish previously cooked and flaked. Sprinkle with paprika and add some more oil and salt if necessary. Let the mixture simmer very gently (but not boil) for about 15 minutes.

Serve this mixture on croutons and sprinkle with parsley.

VI   <u>Salmon in Wine.</u>

    4 thick salmon steaks.
    3/4 cup dry white wine.
    1/4 cup cream.
    2 tablespoons butter.
    1 tablespoon flour.
    Salt, pepper, one onion.

 Bake or broil the steaks. Salt and pepper. Sauté the minced onion in hot butter. Stir in the flour and add the wine and cream, salt and pepper. A bouillon cube added to the sauce improves its flavor.

Saumon

VII   Salmon Loaf.

Can be made with either fresh, left over or canned salmon.

Empty can of salmon into a saucepan and let it come to a boil; drain it, remove skin and bones and cut it up fine. Mix with one and a half cups of Bechamel sauce and 3 very well beaten eggs. Turn into a buttered baking dish. Bake in a moderate oven for 45 minutes. Turn out on a platter and pour a hot tomato sauce around it.

VIII   Fish Soufflé.

    1 lb. cooked fish.
    5 egg yolks.
    6 egg whites.
    1 tablespoon butter.
    1 cup Bechamel sauce.

Cut up the fish very fine. If cod fish is used, put it through a grinder. In a large baking dish stir together the Bechamel and the fish. Add the beaten egg yolks, then fold in the whites beaten stiff. Cover the top with dots of butter. Bake about 45 minutes.

IX   Fish entrée.

To use up any kind of left over fish. Flake it and mix it with a Bechamel or Mornay sauce. Place the mixture in buttered individual baking dishes or large scallop shells. Sprinkle with dots of butter and cheese and brown in oven.

X   Sea Food with Wine.

1 can of shrimps.
1 can of crab meat or lobster meat.
1 pound fresh mushrooms.
3 tablespoons of butter.
1-1/2 cup dry white wine.
A dash of cayenne, salt, white pepper.

Flake the crab or lobster meat and let it absorb most of the juice or liquor from the cans. Don't peel the mushrooms unless very large. Cut in slices and sauté in butter.

Melt the butter in a saucepan, add flour and blend. Add wine and seasoning.

Turn the fish and the sauce into a buttered baking dish, sprinkle with bread crumbs and dots of butter. Brown in the oven.

XI   Fish Salad.

After removing the skin and bones flake the left over fish. In a deep salad bowl cut slices or cubes of boiled potatoes. Season with tarragon, shallots, oil and vinegar. Add some mayonaise and mix the fish and potatoes well. Serve this dish on luttuce leaves garnished with hard boiled eggs 3 or 4 hours after it has been prepared.

XI'I   LOBSTER CROQUETTES

1 quart lobster meat
2 1/2 cups rich cream sauce.
2 eggs.
1 cup sherry.
cracker crumbs.
salt, pepper.
deep fat.

Boil lobsters. Pick out meat and cut into small pieces,
then chill. (Do not chop lobster meat.) Add the sherry.

Make thick rich cream sauce. Scald milk with celery
leaves and a slice of onion which are removed after milk
has scalded.

Pour hot sauce over cold lobster meat. Blend together,
spread mixture in shallow pan and chill.   This is necessary
in order to shape croquettes more easily.

Shape croquettes, roll lightly in prepared cracker crumbs,
dip croquettes in slightly beaten eggs which have been thinned
with one tablespoonful of water, roll in crumbs again and fry in
deep fat until golden brown. Drain on brown paper.

These may be made in advance then placed in a pan lined
with brown paper, and heated before serving. Or the croquettes
may be prepared in advance and fried just before serving.

This makes eighteen medium size croquettes.

The above recipe has been supplied through the kindness
of Mrs. Rupert Baxter of Bath, Maine, and although it is not
of French origin, its excellence is sufficient to win for it a
place of honor in any cook book.

BEEF

I   Beef Chateaubriand.

3 lbs. pot roast beef.
10 small onions.
10 small carrots.
1 tablespoon tomato paste.
1 clove garlic. 1 shallot.
1 tablespoon butter.
1 cup dry white wine.
1/2 cup madeira.
1 liqueur glass brandy.
salt, pepper.

Brown the meat on both sides in butter. Remove meat from the pan. Brown the thinly sliced onions and carrots. Grind the garlic and shallot into a pulp and rub it into the meat. Put all ingredients together into pressure cooker, placing meat on trivet and cook for 30 minutes at 15 lb. pressure. Let pointer return to off position.

If not cooked in a pressure cooker use a dutch oven, cooking slowly for three hours.

II   <u>Boeuf</u> <u>Bourguignon</u>.   (serves 6 or 8)

2 lbs. beef cut in small pieces.
1/4 lb. fat back cut in cubes.
1/2 lb. mushrooms.
1 1/2 cup red wine.
2 cups consommé.
1 tablespoonful butter
1 tablespoonful flour.
Thyme. Bay leaf. Salt. Pepper.
12 small onions.

Melt butter in a dutch oven and brown first the cubes of fat back and the onions. Put them on a dish and next cook the sliced mushrooms. Remove the mushrooms and brown the meat. Sprinkle the flour over the meat and stir. When the flour has become a nice golden brown add the wine and consommé. Put all the ingredients together in dutch oven. Season and cover. Cook slowly 2 to 2 1/2 hours. If done in a pressure cooker, place the meat on trivet and cook 25 minutes at 15 lbs. pressure. Let pointer return to off position.

Boeuf Bourguignon

III   Boeuf Miroton.

In order to serve left over beef as a new dish make the following sauce.

Brown two thinly sliced onions in one tablespoon of butter. Sprinkle one tablespoon of flour and when it turns brown add 1/2 cup of white wine and one cup of consommé. Cook slowly for 15 minutes. Add the meat cut into thin slices. After the meat is in the sauce do not let it boil but only simmer just long enough to heat the meat. Just before serving add a teaspoonful of good wine vinegar. You can also slice a few pickles into the sauce.

IV   Steak a la Bordelaise.

This is a thick steak broiled in the usual manner but served as follows:

Blend a third of a stick of softened butter with finely chopped parsley, chives and shallots. Form into a walnut shaped ball.

When the steak is done season it and put it on the serving platter. Place the butter on it and leave the dish in the oven for a minute or two.

V   Goulache

2 lbs. beef cut in 1 1/2 inch cubes.
1/4 lb. fat back cut in cubes.
6 large onions
1 cup consommé or water.
1 teaspoon paprika
1 tablespoon butter or bacon fat.
salt, pepper, 1 dash cayenne.

Melt butter in pan and brown fat back and onions sliced fine. Next brown meat and put all ingredients together. Add seasoning and paprika. Cover meat with consommé or water. If consommé is used much less salt is needed.

Cook slowly in dutch oven for 2 1/2 hours, or 15 minutes at 15 lbs pressure in pressure cooker.

VI   Italian Stufata

2 lbs. beef pot roast.
1/2 lb. fat back.
1 lb. of onions, carrots, turnips.
1 handful mushrooms.
1 bottle Chianti.
Thyme. bay leaf, salt, pepper.

Marinate in the wine over night the meat, with half the
fat back, the vegetables, thyme, bay leaf.

When ready to prepare drain and dry the meat and
vegetables. Reserve the wine. Melt the remaining half
of fat back in dutch oven or pressure cooker. Brown meat
on all sides. Brown vegetables and mushrooms. Return
all ingredients to the pan and pour over the wine. Season
to taste, cover and cook very slowly for four hours if dutch
oven is used. Cook 25 minutes at 15 lbs. pressure in pressure cooker.

Chianti

Stufato italienne

VII   Beef Tongue   (fresh or smoked)

Soak tongue in cold water for several hours. Then
cook it for half an hour in salted boiling water. Take the
tongue out and remove the skin. Place in a saucepan a
tablespoon of butter or bacon fat and brown the tongue in
it. Then add a carrot sliced fine, four tomatoes quartered ,
peeled and seeded, 2/3 of a cup of white wine. Cover and
cook for three hours if using a dutch oven, or 35 minutes in
pressure cooker on trivet. Slice the tongue and pour the
sauce over it. If when ready to serve, the sauce is too thin
uncover the pan and let boil hard for a few minutes. If, on
the other hand the sauce is too thick add some water or
consommé. Taste and rectify seasoning.

Langue de boeuf

VEAL

I   Veal Marengo   (for 6)

3 lbs. of breast of veal cut in cubes.
3/4 cup oil.
1 large onion.
1 scant tablespoon flour.
3/4 cup white wine.
2 cups stock or water.
2 lbs. tomatoes or 3/4 cup tomatoe paste.
1 clove garlic.
1/4 lb. mushrooms.
1 tablespoonful minced parsley.
salt, pepper.

Veau Marengo

Put the oil in a large skillet or a dutch oven. Heat it
well and brown the pieces of meat on all sides. If there
are too many pieces of meat do not put them all in at
once as they must all be well browned all over. When
they are done take them out and put in the minced onion.
When transparent sprinkle the flour and allow to brown.
Then add the stock and wine and when it begins to boil
put in the garlic, tomatoes (peeled and seeded) salt and
pepper, meat and mushrooms sliced. Cover and cook in
the oven about 2 hours.

When ready turn out on a platter sprinkle with minced
parsley and surround with croutons.

Some people prefer this dish without wine in this case
add more stock.

II   Veal Paprika

2 veal steaks. 1 lb. each.
1 onion
1/2 cup sour cream.
1/2 cup stock or water.
mushrooms if available.
paprika, salt and pepper.

In a pressure cooker or a dutch oven put a tablespoon
of crisco or butter. When very hot shake some paprika into
it and brown the meat well on all sides. Take out the meat
and brown the minced onion and mushrooms. Put everything together in pressure cooker placing meat on trivet.
Add the sour cream and stock. Season to taste and cook at
15 lbs. pressure for 10 minutes.

If this dish is done in dutch oven cook for 2 hours.

III   Blanquette of Veal

    2 1/2 pounds of shoulder of veal. (cubed)
    3 onions , 2 cloves garlic.
    3 shallots, 2 carrots.
    parsley, bay leaf, salt, pepper.
    3 tablespoons butter.
    2 tablespoons flour.
    3/4 pint of veal stock.
    6 tablespoons cream.
    2 egg yolks
    juice of one lemon.

Place the meat and vegetables in one quart of cold salted
water and bring to a boil. Skim the water to remove the scum
and let it simmer for 2 hours. Reserve the liquid for sauce.

    In a saucepan melt the butter and if you have any mush-
rooms sauté them in the butter. Sprinkle the flour and stir
until light golden brown. Add the 3/4 pint of strained veal
stock. In a bowl mix the egg yolks and lemon juice and add
this mixture to the sauce being careful not to let it boil.
Season to taste.

    Place the drained pieces of meat on a deep serving platter
and pour the sauce over them. Add the cream at the last
moment.

    This dish goes very well with rice. It can be kept hot in a
double boiler.

IV   Veal cutlets á la Maréchale.

10 veal cutlets
1 , cup chopped ham
1 1/2 cup of fat back
1/2 lb. of mushrooms
2 cloves of garlic. 1 bunch parsley.
3 shallots, salt, pepper, allspice.

Put two tablespoons of butter or crisco in a large and shallow earthenware dish. Brown the cutlets on both sides. Season with salt and pepper.

Make a stuffing with ham, fat back, mushrooms, garlic, parsley etc. Season.

Place the stuffing over the cutlets and pour into the dish 1 1/2 cup of Madeira sauce. Recipe on page 7 . Sprinkle bread crumbs and butter on top and finish the cooking in the oven. Serve in the same dish.

V.   Veal Birds.

Veal steaks	=	2 lbs.
Sausage meat	=	1/4 lb.
Beaten egg	=	1
Butter	=	1 heaping tablespoon.
Consommé	=	1 cup.
Bread crumbs	=	1 tablespoonful dipped in milk.

Make a stuffing with sausage meat, bread crumbs, the egg, parsley. Add pepper and a little salt. Cut the veal steaks into thin serving pieces. Spread some stuffing onto each piece of veal and roll it up neatly. (You can roll a strip of bacon around each veal bird). Fasten with skewer or string. Heat butter in pressure cooker and brown the veal birds on all sides. Add consommé and cook 12 minutes at 15 lbs. pressure. Let pointer return to off position. Thicken gravy with flour if necessary.

VI.   <u>Breaded Veal Steaks.</u>

2 lbs. veal steak - 1 inch thick.
1 cup bread crumbs.
1/2 cup flour.
1 egg.
2 tablespoons butter.

Place three plates in front of you. The first containing the
flour mixed with salt and pepper, the second containing the
beaten egg and the third the bread crumbs.

Cut the veal into serving pieces then dip each piece first in
the flour, next in the egg, last in the bread crumbs.

Melt the butter in the pressure cooker and sear the meat well
on both sides. Replace trivet in pressure cooker and arrange
pieces of meat over it. Cover with one cup Béchamel sauce well
seasoned. As the Béchamel sauce does not afford enough mois-
ture put 1/2 cup of milk or water under the trivet.

Cover and cook 12 minutes at 15 lbs. pressure. In a dutch oven
cook 1 1/2 hours.

VII.   Fricandeau.

    3 lbs. veal.
    10 strips bacon.
    1 onion
    1 carrot
    parsley, thyme, bay leaf.
    1 cup white wine.
    3 cups stock or consommé or water.

In the bottom of a Dutch oven or a pressure cooker arrange five strips of bacon and on the bacon the sliced onion and carrot, parsley, thyme, bay leaf. On top of these place the veal cut in serving pieces. Cover and cook very slowly for 20 minutes without touching it or lifting the cover. Then add the wine and consommé so that the meat is barely covered. If the cooking is done in a Dutch oven bring to a boil, cover, and cook slowly for 3 hours in a slow oven. In the pressure cooker cook 30 minutes.

When the meat is done it should be tender enough to be cut with a spoon.

Before serving remove the excess fat from the sauce.

Fricandeau

VIII   Calf's feet in jelly.

Buy one or two calf's feet and ask the butcher to split
them in two lengthwise and then in four pieces the other way.
Each foot should be thus in four pieces. Wash them then place
in a saucepan with cold salted water. Bring to a boil. Remove the scum. Add some turnips, carrots and leeks. Let
it simmer for four hours. Then take the meat out and throw
away the bones and muscles which have become separated in
cooking. Arrange the pieces of meat in a mold. Color the
stock with a few drops of caramel or any other way you may
prefer. Taste it and rectify seasoning. Strain the stock through
a fine sieve and pour into the mold over the pieces of meat.
Place in refrigerator over night and serve with a well seasoned
mayonnaise.

This makes an excellent dish in summer.

IX   Calf's brains in white wine.

    1 brain.
    5 or 6 slices of onion.
    5 or 6 slices of carrot.
    parsley, thyme, bay leaf, 2 cloves.
    1 1/2 cup white wine.
    1 cup consommé.
    1 tablespoon butter.
    1 scant tablespoon flour.
    1 egg yolk.
    juice one lemon.

First wash brains, remove arteries and membranes and
soak one hour in cold water. In a small saucepan arrange
the brains on a layer formed with the onion, carrot, bay leaf
etc., and a dash of nutmeg. Pour wine and consommé over
it and bring to a boil. Simmer for 25 minutes and drain reserv-
ing the liquid. Keep brains warm and covered. Strain liquid
through a fine sieve.

In another saucepan place half your butter and work the flour
into it. Add the strained liquid which should measure 1 1/2 cups.
Let it simmer 4 or 5 minutes. Take it off the fire and just before pouring it onto the brains add the rest of the butter, the egg
yolk and lemon juice. Taste for seasoning before serving.

Cervelle au vin blanc

X   Calf's brains in butter.

First wash and prepare brain (if the butcher has not done it)
and soak it for an hour. Then put it in a saucepan and cover it
with water. Add salt, a spoonful of vinegar and a sprig of parsley.
When the water comes to a boil the brain is cooked. Melt some
butter in a baking dish until it becomes light brown. Add the well
drained brains. Sprinkle with salt, pepper, fine bread crumbs
and dots of butter. Bake for 10 minutes. Sprinkle minced parsley
over it before serving and serve with lemon.

KIDNEYS.

Allow 2 lamb kidneys per person and one veal kidney for
two persons.

Wash in cold water, remove skin and cut kidneys into slices.

Put in skillet one tablespoon butter or bacon fat. Fry in it
one large onion or two small ones sliced. When the onion has
become transparent add the sliced kidneys and cook, turning them
all the time with a spoon, 7 or 8 minutes. Kidneys must not be
overcooked as they become hard. When kidneys are done sprinkle
over them a spoonful of flour stir it in well and add 1/2 cup of
white wine or more as desired. If this dish is not to be served
immediately keep it hot in a double boiler or over a very low
flame but do not let it boil.

LAMB

I   Braised Leg of Lamb.

This recipe can be done very well in the pressure cooker.

Sauté the leg of lamb in butter and turn it so as to brown it on all sides. Break the bone if necessary but cook the bone with the meat. Sprinkle salt and pepper on the leg of lamb while it is browning. Place the meat on trivet in pressure cooker and add a cup and a half of white wine and twelve cloves of garlic. If the leg of lamb weighs from three to five pounds cook 30 minutes at 15 lbs. pressure. Before serving add the juice of a lemon to the sauce in which the taste of garlic is not recognizable.

This is especially good for cooking a shoulder of lamb which is a tougher cut of meat. Ask the butcher to remove the bones and roll the meat but cook bones with meat.

Gigot à l'ail

II   Grilled Kidneys.

Soak in cold water, remove skin. Split kidneys open but
do not separate the two halves. Arrange them on metal skewers
so that they will remain flat. Brush oil over them and sprinkle
with salt and pepper. Place under broiler presenting the inside
to the flame first. Broil 3 minutes on each side. Remove skewers
from broiler and before serving place on each half of kidney a dot
of butter mixed with chopped chives, shallots and parsley.

III   Cassoulet.

The real Cassoulet of Castelnaudary calls for goose meat
and goose fat but in their absence the following ingredients can
be used.

     1 lb. shoulder of lamb cut in small pieces.
     1/2 lb. fresh pork.
     1/4 lb. fat back.
     1/2 lb. link sausage.
     1/2 lb. Italian sausage. (salami)
     1 pint navy beans.
     10 cloves garlic.
     1 lb. tomatoes.

Soak navy beans for a few hours. Then place in cold water
with salt and bring to a boil. Cook until almost done adding
boiling water when necessary so as to always have plenty of
liquid with the beans.

Put butter or crisco (or goose fat) in a saucepan and brown
the meat and fat back. Remove meat and fat back and in the
same saucepan cook tomatoes and minced garlic. When done to
a purée add salt and pepper and strain. Cook the sausage and cut
into small pieces. Slice the Italian sausage into thin slices,
removing the skin.

In a deep baking dish arrange layers of beans, meat, fat back, sausages. With the beans put some of the water in which they have cooked as there must be plenty of liquid. Over the top layer pour the tomato purée and some of the fat from the sausages. Top with a sprinkling of bread crumbs and finish cooking in the oven until the beans are quite done.

This dish requires a lengthy preparation but it makes a wonderful pièce de résistance for a meal or a buffet supper and it can be reheated and served several times. If in the course of cooking or reheating it should become too dry add some hot water or consommé. Do not forget plenty of salt and pepper.

Cassoulet -

PORK

Most French people use garlic with pork. A roast pork well larded with 4 or 5 cloves of garlic has a much better flavor.

I   Pork chops peasant style.

Use pork chops or steaks.

Sauté the meat in a skillet. When done remove meat and throw into skillet a handful of chopped shallots. 2 or 3 minutes is enough to brown shallots. Add a tablespoon of good wine vinegar and pour contents of skillet over the meat.

II   Pork chops, Mexican style.

    6 pork chops.
    6 tablespoons rice.
    1 onion, sliced.
    1 tomato, sliced.
    3 1/2 cups consommé.

Sauté chops on both sides. Remove from skillet and brown onion and rice in the skillet. Place the chops at the bottom of a deep earthenware casserole. Cover with rice, the sliced tomato and the consommé.   Cover dish and simmer in a slow oven about one hour.

III   <u>Pig's feet.</u>

Broiled pig's feet are delicious and very easy to prepare.
Buy them already boiled. Brush them well with melted butter.
Sprinkle with salt and pepper, roll in fine bread crumbs and
broil under low flame about 12 or 15 minutes. Allow one foot
per person.

IV   <u>Pork á la Catalane.</u>

It is a roast served with Sauce Soubise as given on page 7 ,
that is to say a purée of onions.

CHICKEN

The usual way in France, and also the most simple way to treat a chicken when it is young and tender is to roast it in the oven sometimes with stuffing, very often without. When roasting it without stuffing proceed as follows:

Take a good spoonful of butter, soft enough to be able to blend with it 1/2 a spoonful of chopped parsley or chopped tarragon. Place it inside the chicken with salt and pepper. Brush the chicken all over with melted butter, salt and pepper. Place in baking dish in moderate oven as chicken must cook slowly and thoroughly. Remove chicken from baking dish and mix two or three spoonfuls of hot water or bouillon with the fat in the pan.

If a stuffing is used it is made with:

    the liver from the chicken chopped fine.
    sausage meat. (cooked)
    some bread crumbs dipped in milk or bouillon.
    parsley, salt, pepper.
    one egg.
    mushrooms or chestnuts added to the stuffing are a
    a great improvement.

Poulet rôti

I   <u>Poulet Marengo.</u>

1 chicken, cut as for frying.
4 tablespoonfuls olive oil.
3 large tomatoes.
1 dozen small mushrooms.
1 cup bouillon.
1/2 cup white wine.
1 clove garlic.
1 tablespoonful chopped parsley.
1 scant tablespoon butter mixed with
1 teaspoon flour.
salt, pepper.

Heat oil in heavy frying pan and cook chicken until nicely browned. Keep a moderate fire and do not cover pan. It should take 20 or 25 minutes. Remove chicken onto a hot platter. Pour the oil into a small skillet which will be used later to fry croutons.

In the frying pan put the peeled and seeded tomatoes, minced garlic, wine, bouillon and the mushrooms wiped and sliced if too large. Let it boil down to about one cup liquid, then mix with it the butter and flour. Salt and pepper.

Reheat the chicken in the sauce but do not let it boil. Serve with croutons and sprinkled with parsley.

II   <u>Poulet Périgourdine.</u>

1 chicken, cut for frying
1/2 tablespoon crisco.
1 tablespoonful of fat back, cubed.
1 onion with cloves.
1 scant tablespoon flour.
3 lbs. oyster plant, sliced but not too thin.
salt, pepper.
one pint bouillon.

Put the crisco in a heavy frying pan and fry first the fat back and onion. Remove from pan and fry the chicken. Remove chicken and fry oyster plant. Remove oyster plant and keep in frying pan only about one tablespoon of fat. Sprinkle flour stirring with a wooden spoon. When the flour becomes golden add a pint of bouillon slowly stirring all the time. Strain the liquid and put it with the chicken and oyster plant cubes of fat back, onion and a few sprigs of parsley and bay leaf tied together. Simmer gently for 2 hours.

Serve only chicken and oyster plant and remove excess fat from sauce if necessary.

If the cooking is done in the pressure cooker 12 or 15 minutes at 15 lbs. pressure is enough.

poulet ____

III   <u>Coq au vin.</u>

Cut the chicken as for frying.

In a good frying pan put three tablespoons of olive oil
and 7 or 8 cubes of fat back. Fry the chicken until golden
brown all over. Sprinkle with a good spoonful of flour. When
flour browns add about two cups of a dry white wine (enough to
cover chicken). Add 3 cloves of garlic mashed very fine, one
bay leaf, 1/2 lb. of mushrooms sliced. Cover and simmer for
about one hour. Season to taste.

Coq au vin

IV   Chicken á la Normande.

Cut the chicken as for frying. Put it in a saucepan with a
spoonful of butter, one carrot, one onion with cloves, thyme,
parsley, bay leaf, and 1/4 lb. of fat back. Cover with cold
water and bring to a boil. Remove scum several times during
first half hour. When chicken is done take it out of the saucepan and boil the liquid down to one cup. Strain it and add one
cup of milk, salt, pepper, chopped tarragon.

In a bowl mix together 1/2 cup heavy cream the yolk of an
egg and some spoonfuls of the sauce. Put everything together,
taste for seasoning and keep warm if necessary in a double boiler.

V   Squab or Quail Catalane.

Brown birds well in crisco. Remove from frying pan and
replace with one onion sliced. When onion is almost done add
one minced clove of garlic. Then half a cup of diced ham, one
tablespoon of tomato paste. Simmer all these ingredients together for 10 or 15 minutes. Add next 1/2 cup water, salt and
pepper. Put the birds back in the pan and simmer everything
together.

In a saucepan boil together 4 cloves of garlic and a sliced
lemon. You can mash the garlic if desired and leave it in the
sauce or take it out. Add garlic and lemon 15 minutes before
serving.

In Spain and Southern France the lemon is replaced with
sour oranges which give a better flavor.

MEAT LOAVES

I   Pâté de Lapin. (Rabbit Pie)

For a rabbit weighing almost 2 lbs. take:

        3/4 lb. fresh pork.
        1/2 lb. fat back.
        1/2 lb. cooked ham.
        1/2 cup dry white wine.
        salt (almost 3 teaspoonful).
        allspice (almost 1 teaspoon).

Take the rabbit's meat off the bones. Set aside the kidneys
and all the meat that can be cut into fairly large strips (all the
meat off the back and the legs).

Melt a few pieces of fat back in a frying pan and sauté very
slightly in it the large strips of rabbit's meat. Remove and
place into a deep dish together with 1/2 the remaining fat back
and the ham, both diced. Cover with the wine and 1/4 of the
salt and spices. Marinate 1 hour.

Sauté the liver. Put it together with the fresh pork, remaining fat back and all that is left over of the rabbit's meat. Add the remaining salt and allspice and put through meat grinder, grinding very fine. Line the bottom of a baking dish with strips of bacon or very thin pieces of fat back. Fill the baking dish with alternating layers of ground meat and marinated strips of meat. Pour the remaining wine over everything, top with a few strips of bacon, cover the dish and place in the oven in a pan of boiling water. The boiling water must be replaced during the cooking and always reach to about 1/3 of the baking dish.

Cook in a moderate oven for 1 1/2 hour or 2 hours. The bacon is optional. If bacon is used less salt is needed.

Instead of fresh pork, sausage meat can be used.

II   Ham and Veal Loaf.

1/2 lb. lean veal
1/2 lb. uncooked ham.
1/4 lb. fat back.

In addition, for the stuffing 1/2 lb. veal and 1/2 lb. sausage meat ground and mixed with salt, pepper, allspice.

Arrange in baking dish as for the preceding rabbit's pie and cook in the same manner. Cook in moderate oven allowing 35 minutes for each pound of meat.

Before beginning to bake the meat loaf pour over it 1/2 cup of consommé if no bacon strips are placed on top.

III   Pork Liver and Meat Loaf.

        2 lbs pork meat.
        1 lb. pork liver
        1/2 lb. fat salt pork. (or more if meat is very lean.)
        6 cloves garlic.
        1 handful parsley.
        2 teaspoon salt.
        1 teaspoon allspice.
        thyme, bay leaf.
        strips bacon.

    Grind all ingredients together and season well. Arrange
in baking dish. Cover with strips of bacon. Cover dish and
bake in a pan of boiling water in a moderate oven for 1 1/2
hours.

IV   Pork Liver Loaf.

        1 lb. pork liver.
        1 lb. fat back
        6 cloves of garlic.
        1 1/2 teaspoon salt
        1/2 teaspoon allspice.
        1 sprig of thyme, bay leaf.

    Grind all ingredients together, season and turn into baking
dish. Cover dish and bake for 1 1/2 hours in a moderate oven
being careful to place dish in a pan of boiling water and to re-
fill with more boiling water as it evaporates.

VEGETABLES

I   Stuffed Tomatoes.

Take the desired number of tomatoes choosing them big
and firm and fresh.

Hollow them out on the stem end. Press slightly to expell
water and seeds. Place the part you have scooped out in the
mincing bowl together with five cloves of garlic, a handful of
parsley, one onion, two handfuls of bread crumbs, six strips
of bacon, one egg, salt and pepper. Salt and pepper tomatoes
and fill with above stuffing. Pour some olive oil into a large
and shallow baking dish. Arrange tomatoes in it and start
cooking over open flame with dish covered, for about 15 minutes. Then put the dish in the oven for one hour basting often.
When well baked and golden replace the dish on open flame to
reduce the juice and baste again.

Serve immediately in the same dish.

II   Tomatoes with Cheese.

Take some medium sized ripe tomatoes. Cut in half and
press slightly to expell water and seeds. Arrange in a buttered
shallow baking dish. Sprinkle over the tomatoes, salt, pepper,
chopped shallots, bread crumbs, grated cheese. Pour over it
all some melted butter and bake in moderate oven. Serve in
same dish.

III   <u>Egg Plant á la Castillane.</u>

Cut in slices one inch thick four or five egg plants of medium
size. Boil them 7 or 8 minutes in salt water. Drain and put
on a tea towel to dry.

Peel, seed and quarter, 2 lbs. of tomatoes. Cut two onions
very fine and brown them in two table spoonfuls of olive oil, add
the tomatoes, one clove of garlic, parsley, bay leaf, spices, salt
and pepper and let it cook covered for about 10 minutes over
a slow fire; then take the cover off and cook it fast stirring
all the time to obtain a thick purée.

Oil an earthenware dish and spread into it a layer of egg
plant, then a layer of tomato purée. Sprinkle with grated
gruyére or Parmesan then with a table spoonful of olive oil. Keep
on alternating layers and finish with the purée. Top with cheese,
butter and bread crumbs.

Put in a moderate oven for 40 minutes.

Aubergines farcies —

IV   Cauliflower Gratiné.

Soak cauliflower head down for 30 minutes in cold water.
Cook in boiling salted water until done. The cooking time in
an open saucepan is about 20 minutes and in a pressure cooker
5 minutes.

Separate into flowerets. Place in a baking dish, pour mornay
sauce over it and bake in oven until brown on top.

V   Cauliflower Arlequin.

Cook in salted water, rice, potatoes, cauliflower. Take
the same weight of each and mash with a fork. Mix with it a
good cup or one and a half cup of Mornay sauce. Put in a baking
dish; sprinkle butter and cheese on top and bake until the top
forms a golden crust.

VI   Stuffed Cabbage.

The preparation of this dish takes a long time but its
success is ample reward. Also the preparation comes several
hours before serving time, can even be done the day before.

Take a large cabbage, about 2 lbs. For the stuffing you
can use any kind of left over meat. The fat end of a ham
provides the best kind of stuffing. If ham is used, 3/4 lbs.
meat is needed. If lean meat is used take 1/2 lb. meat and
1/4 lb. fat back. Grind the meat together with a good handful
of parsley and 6 cloves garlic. Mix well with an egg and add
salt and pepper using your own judgement as to quantity needed
according to the kind of meat you have used.

Prepare the cabbage as follows:

Remove the frayed outside leaves. Put in salted boiling water and cook about 15 minutes. Take it out and squeeze it to drain the water. Open the leaves and remove the center part. Insert the stuffing in the center and also between the leaves as much as possible. Tie the cabbage with strings so as to give it its original shape. When it is thus prepared it can wait until the next day.

To cook it place it with some bouillon in a Dutch oven and cook slowly in the oven for 4 hours.

In the pressure cooker, place cabbage on trivet, put in one and a half cup of bouillon and cook 35 minutes. Let pointer return to off position.

To serve remove strings, place in serving dish, pour sauce over it. Slice the cabbage from the center so as to give each person some stuffing as well as cabbage.

VII   Leeks and Potatoes.

Use only the white part of leeks. Slice leeks and potatoes and put in a saucepan alternating layers of leeks and potatoes. Add salt and pepper and enough bouillon or water to cover vegetables. Cook clowly and add butter when serving.

VIII   <u>Beans</u>. (Navy, kidney, etc.)

Allow one pound of shelled beans for 4 of fresh beans,
cook in boiling water. If dry beans, start in cold water. While
the beans are cooking, and their cooking requires about 4 hours,
keep a kettle of boiling water on the stove so as to add to the
beans when needed.

In the meat grinder or in a chopping bowl put together 6
strips of bacon (fat) 6 cloves of garlic and a good handful of
parsley. Grind or chop together and add to the beans one hour
before serving. Season to taste. If desired a tomato or a half
tablespoonful of tomato paste may be added.

This dish usually accompanies a roast leg of lamb.

IX   <u>Green Peas</u>.

      1 pint fresh green peas.
      2 tablespoons butter.
      1 heart of lettuce
      5 or 6 small onions.
      1 small bunch parsley.
      3 lumps sugar.
      1/2 cup water.
      salt, pepper.

Place all ingredients together in a saucepan being careful
to tie together the parsley and lettuce so as to be able to remove it easily before serving. Cook slowly for an hour and
a half keeping the pan covered with a soup plate full of water.
Keep boiling water in a kettle to add to the peas if they become
too dry.

X   Oyster Plant.

Oyster plant is a root vegetable much more used in France
than in the United States. It has a very delicate flavor and
deserves to be better known.

Scrape the oyster plant and throw it into cold acidulated
water to keep it from turning black. Cook until tender in a
large quantity of salted boiling water.

They can be used then to accompany roast meat or prepared in the following manner:

a) Put a good tablespoon of butter in a saucepan and the
sliced and already cooked oyster plant. Sprinkle a good spoonful of parsley on top and toss everything together until the oyster
plant has absorbed the butter.

b) Place the cooked oyster plant in a baking dish. Cover
with mornay sauce and bake until brown on top.

XI   Carrots Vichy.

Slice the carrots rather thin and sauté in butter. Add salt
and pepper and a few minutes before serving sprinkle a good
teaspoon of granulated sugar or brown sugar over the carrots
tossing them well in the pan in order to have them all coated
with sugar.

XII   Leeks   Gratiné

Take three pounds of leeks and cut them in slices about
an inch thick using only the white part. Cook 15 minutes in
boiling salted water. Drain well and put in a baking dish with
2 cups of sauce Béchamel or sauce mornay. Cover the top with
bread crumbs and dots of butter and bake for 15 or 20 minutes.

XIII   Potatoe Soufflé.   (for 8)

Take four large potatoes, about a pound or more. One
tablespoonful of butter, one cup of milk or cream, 4 egg yolks,
6 egg whites.

Boil potatoes and having mashed them through food mill mix
well with butter and milk adding salt and pepper and a pinch of nutmeg. Then add the egg yolks and when the mixture is almost cold
the stiffly beaten egg whites. Turn into baking dish and brush the
top with butter in order to obtain a glaze. Bake in a slow oven
25 minutes.

pommes de terre Dauphines

XIV   Potatoes Dauphinoise (with cheese)

     1 lb. potatoes.
     2 cups milk.
     2 eggs.
     3 heaping tablespoons cheese.

Peel the potatoes and slice them. Arrange in a baking dish alternating layers of potatoes and cheese and sprinkle with salt and pepper.

Break the eggs into a bowl and beat them with the milk. Add some salt and pepper but not too much. Remember cheese is salted. Pour this mixture in the baking dish and bake in a slow oven for about an hour or until the top forms a golden crust.

XV   Potatoes Southern Style.

Peel and slice potatoes. In a heavy skillet melt a tablespoon of Crisco or butter and when it is very hot put potatoes into skillet. Stir potatoes very often and when they are almost done add a handful of parsley and three cloves of garlic chopped very fine. Salt and serve on a hot platter.

XVI   Salad Dressing.

French salad dressing is very simple but it requires some herbs in order to be really good. Some chives or tarragon chopped up fine in the dressing improve it a hundred percent.

At the bottom of a salad bowl put 2 pinches of salt, one of pepper, one or two tablespoons of vinegar and three tablespoons of oil. Salt melts in vinegar and not in oil. Therefore be sure to mix the salt in the vinegar before adding the oil. One small teaspoon full of powdered mustard may be added if desired. Or the crushed yolk of a hard boiled egg.*

This dressing accompanies all salads and vegetables such as artichokes, cauliflowers, leeks, beets and tomatoes which can be served either as salads or hors d'oeuvres.

*Instead of mustard and egg mashed Roquéfort cheese can be added.

DESERTS

I   French Custard.

    1 pint milk.
    3/4 cup sugar.
    2 whole eggs.
    4 egg yolks.

Heat the milk together with the flavoring, either vanilla or the rind of half a lemon or half an orange, and the sugar.

In a bowl mix well the two eggs and 4 egg yolks adding a few spoons of the hot milk gradually. Pour the eggs into the milk stirring constantly. Do not let it boil. The custard is ready when the mixture coats the spoon. It is safer to make this custard in a double boiler.

For a thicker and less expensive custard use 2 or 3 eggs only and two teaspoonfuls of cornstarch.

II   Baked Caramel Custard.

    1 pint milk.
    3/4 cup sugar.
    2 or 3 eggs.
    dash of salt, vanilla.

Heat milk and add sugar. Add vanilla and a dash of salt. Pour scalded milk over beaten eggs.

Prepare a caramel by putting two tablespoonfuls of granulated sugar, 2 teaspoons of water in a small skillet. Brown sugar and when golden and liquid pour it into a baking dish twisting the dish so as to caramelize the sides as well as the bottom. Pour the custard into the baking dish and bake in a slow oven in a pan of hot water. Cooking time about 20 minutes. Let it cool and un-mold on a platter or bowl that will allow space for the caramel sauce.

Crème renversée

III   <u>Bavarian Cream.</u>

Prepare a custard as in number I. Flavor it with coffee or chocolate. While it is cooking soak in cold water one tablespoon of granulated gelatin and then dissolve it in the hot custard. Whip up one cup and a quarter of heavy cream and fold into the custard when it is almost cold.   Pour into a mold and chill.

IV   Rice

To cook rice for desserts proceed in the following manner.

    1 cup rice.
    4 cups milk.
    1 1/2 tablespoons sugar.

Scald milk and melt sugar in it. Add flavoring.

Wash rice and put in in a saucepan. Cover with cold water. Bring to a boil and let boil 5 minutes. Put rice in a strainer and wash rapidly with cold water. Drain well and put with milk in a baking dish. Bake in slow oven 35 or 40 minutes or until rice is soft.

V   Rice Cake.

Cook rice as indicated in preceding recipe. Then fold into it one tablespoon butter and when mixture is cool enough 2 eggs, the whites beaten stiff. Pour mixture into a caramelized mold and bake in moderate oven in a pan of water. Serve with vanilla or lemon custard.

VI   Pouding Macédoine.

Soak in 1/2 cup of rum 1/2 lb. of candied orange peels, citron, angelica and 6 tablespoonfuls of currents and seeded raisins. Make a custard as in No. 1 and add to it one envelope of gelatine and 1/4 lb. of crushed macaroons. Pour all ingredients together in a mold and chill.

VII   Pouding Parisienne.

Prepare a coffee custard (No. 1) Set aside a cup and a quarter of it.

In the still warm custard mix two envelopes of gelatine and when the custard is cold 5 tablespoons of heavy cream.

Slice some lady fingers lengthwise and soak them in 3 tablespoonfuls of rum or kirsch mixed with 2 tablespoons of sugar. Butter a mold and line the bottom of it with a layer of lady fingers. Then put in a layer of the custard and keep on alternating the layers and placing between each some candied orange and citron peels. Chill for a few hours and unmold on a platter. Serve using as a sauce the custard that has been set aside.

Pouding Parisienne

VIII   <u>Pouding á la maréchale.</u>

1 pint custard (No. 1) vanilla.
1/4 lb. of crushed macaroons.
1/4 lb. lady fingers.
1/4 lb. seeded raisins.
grated rind of 1/2 lemon.
Some candied orange peel and citron cut in small cubes.

Before custard cools add to it two envelopes of gelatine.
Arrange all ingredients in baking dish and pour slowly the still
warm custard over it.. Chill a few hours and unmold.

Serve with whipped cream or a fruit sauce.

IX   <u>Rice à l' Impératrice.</u>

1 pint of milk .
4 tablespoons rice.
6 tablespoons sugar.
4 eggs.
1/2 cup heavy cream.
1 dash of salt.
candied orange peel, citron, angelica, seeded raisins
soaked in half a cup of rum.

Cook the rice in half a pint of milk. Make a custard with
the rest of the milk, the eggs, sugar, vanilla. Mix rice and
custard and when mixture is cold fold in the whipped cream.
Butter a mold, pour the mixture into it alternating layers of
mixture and candied fruit. Chill for several hours. To unmold dip mold for a minute or two in boiling water and pudding
will slip out easily.

X   <u>Bread Pudding.</u>

     one loaf of bread.
     one quart of milk.
     one teaspoon vanilla.
     3/4 cup sugar.
     3 eggs.
     1/2 cup seedless raisins.
     1/2 cup malaga raisins.
     1 tablespoon of rum.

Caramel:

     1/2 cup sugar.
     2 teaspoons water.

Sauce:

     3 cups water, currant jelly.
     2 tablespoons of rum.

Caramelize the baking dish.

Scald sweetened milk with vanilla. Crumble the bread in it and work it well with a fork. Beat the whole eggs and add them to the mixture while stirring. 1/4 of a stick of butter added at this point improves the pudding. Add the raisins soaked in the rum. Mix everything well and pour in the caramelized baking dish. Place the dish in a pan of water and cook in a slow oven for about onehour.

Unmold the pudding on a serving dish and serve with a currant jelly sauce.

XI   Vanilla or Chocolate Souffle.

1 cup milk
2 1/2 tablespoonfuls sugar.
1 tablespoonful flour mixed in 3 spoonfuls cold milk.
3 egg yolks.
4 egg whites.
1/2 tablespoonful butter.
1 teaspoon vanilla.

Scald sweetened milk. Add the flour mixed with cold milk.
Bring to a boil, then take off the fire. Add the butter and vanilla.
Let cool and stir in the egg yolks. Last fold in the stiffly beaten
egg whites. Turn into a baking dish and bake at once in a moderate oven for 20 or 25 minutes. Do not fill dish as soufflé will
rise during the cooking. To bake set in a pan of water and, for
a firm soufflé, bake 30 minutes.

Proceed in the same manner for chocolate soufflé folding in 3
squares of melted chocolate before adding the egg yolks. If
bitter chocolate is used add one tablespoon sugar.

crèpes bretonnes

XII   Pan cakes.

In France pan cakes are eaten as dessert, either plain with
sugar or rolled up and stuffed with chocolate mousse or straw-
berry jam. They make a good dish for a Sunday night supper when
everybody is in the kitchen and can take turn at making them.

In a large mixing bowl put the grated rind of a lemon, 2 cups
of flour, a teaspoonful of salt, a tablespoonful of oil and a
tablespoonful of rum or brandy, 4 whole eggs. Mix batter until
smooth and add slowly one cup of milk, and one cup and a quarter
of water.

This makes about 22 pancakes.

The batter can be prepared the day before and if it looks
a little thick add a few tablespoons water.

Make pan cakes very thin in a heavy iron skillet in which you
place first a dot of butter. When done on one side flip pan cake
with spatula and brown on other side.

XIII   Orange Pudding.

        1/2 teaspoonful grated orange rind.
        1 1/2 cups orange juice.
        5 eggs.
        2/3 cup sugar.

Steep orange rind in orange juice for 30 minutes in covered
dish. Mix the eggs well with 1/2 cup sugar. Strain orange juice
and add it slowly to egg mixture stirring all the time. Melt
remaining sugar, adding a few drops of water, in a small
skillet, do not burn. Butter baking dish and line with caramelized
sugar before it hardens. Pour in egg mixture, place in a pan of
warm water and bake in a slow oven about 25 or 30 minutes.

XIV   Viennese Plum Cake.

    1/2 cup butter.
    1/2 cup sugar.
    grated rind 1/2 lemon.
    2 eggs.
    1 cup sifted cake flour.
    1 teaspoon baking powder.
    1/4 teaspoon salt.
    10 nectarines or plums, halved and pitted.

Topping:

    1/2 cup sugar.
    2 teaspoons cinamon.

Cream butter, blend in sugar, add flavoring and beat in eggs one at a time. Add sifted dry ingredients, beat until smooth. Pour into a greased pan (8 x 8 x 2) and press nectarines, skin side down, into batter. Sprinkle with mixed sugar and cinamon. Bake in a moderate oven for about 50 minutes.

XV   Mock Rum Baba.

    3 eggs.
    6 tablespoons bread crumbs
    3 tablespoons sugar.
    2 tablespoons raisins.
    1 teaspoon vanilla.

Mix egg yolks and sugar working them well together. Add bread crumbs and finally, the stiffly beaten egg whites and the raisins. Butter a ring mold and sprinkle enough bread crumbs to dust the mold. Put in moderate oven and cook for 25 minutes.

Sirup:

>one cup water.
>one cup sugar.
>1/2 cup rum.

Cook sugar and water until fairly thick, adding rum in the last few minutes of cooking.

Take baba out of mold when done and pour sirup over it while baba is still warm.

The Real Baba

>11 spoonfuls flour
>1/4 lb. butter. (or a little more.)
>1 teaspoon salt.
>2 tablespoons raisins.
>2 tablespoons baking powder.
>2 tablespoons milk.
>2 tablespoons sugar.
>1 teaspoon vanilla.
>3 eggs.

This must be cooked in a deep ring mold as the batter must, before being cooked, rise to twice its original volume.

In a deep mixing bowl place the baking powder, a spoonful of flour and work with the two tablespoons of milk. When you have a smooth batter leave it alone in the mixing bowl until it has doubled its volume. Then mix the other ingredients with it, the flour, butter, eggs one at a time, sugar and salt and last the raisins. Work the batter well with your hands for about 15 minutes or until air bubbles begin to form. Then pour it into the buttered mold and set aside in a warm place, covered with a tea towel, until the batter has risen to the edge of the mold. Bake in a slow oven for about 45 minutes. Then proceed as in the preceding recipe. Pour sirup over baba and serve with whipped cream.

XVI   Chocolate Mousse

5 eggs.
1/4 lb. butter. (sweet butter)
1/4 lb. sugar.
1/4 lb. chocolate.

Separate the eggs, mix the yolks with sugar and butter. Cream well. Add melted chocolate. Beat the egg whites stiff and fold into mixture. Chill before serving.

This mousse can be made without butter and served with whipped cream. If butter is used it must be sweet butter.

Mousse au chocolat

XVII   <u>Chocolate Charlotte</u>   (for 12)

        2 cups heavy cream.
        1/2 lb. lady fingers.
        1 lb. macaroons.
        1/2 lb. semi-sweet chocolate.
        1 tablespoon sugar.
        1/2 cup rum, 1/2 cup water, mixed.

    Soak lady fingers in rum and water mixture. Line a
charlotte mold, bottom and sides with lady fingers. Melt
chocolate with enough water to be able to spread it. Whip up
cream with sugar and a teaspoon vanilla. In the mold arrange
one layer of crumbled macaroons, one of chocolate, one of
whipped cream. Top with a layer of macaroons (whole) or lady
fingers. Chill for 4 or 5 hours.

    Unmold just before serving.

XVIII   Quatre - Quarts   (or the French equivalent
                                 for pound cake.)

This cake derives its name from the four ingredients
used in equal quantities.

> 4 eggs.
> 1/2 lb. sugar.
> 1/2 lb. butter.
> 1/2 lb. flour.
> grated rind of a lemon.

Work together in a mixing bowl the sugar, egg yolks,
lemon rind. Then add slowly the melted butter, the flour,
working it well into the mixture. Last of all fold in the egg
whites beaten stiff and pour into one or two cake pans,
depending on size.

Bake in slow oven about 30 minutes.

Gâteau

XIX   Chocolate Cake.

1/2 lb. sweet chocolate.
1/4 lb. butter.
3 tablespoonfuls flour
4 eggs
1 teaspoon baking powder

Soften chocolate mixing it with two or three tablespoons of water and stirring with a wooden spoon. Work it into the softened and creamed butter and add the egg yolks then the flour. Last fold in the stiffly beaten egg whites and turn into a buttered cake pan. Cook 25 or 30 minutes in a moderate oven.

When the cake has cooled cover it with coffee or chocolate icing, or white icing.

1)   Chocolate Icing.

On a very low flame or in a double boiler melt 2 squares chocolate with half a tablespoon water. Mix 3 heaping table-spoons confectioner's sugar with 2 spoonfuls of water. With a wooden spoon work the chocolate and sugar together until you obtain a chocolate icing glossy and soft enough to spread.

2)   Coffee Icing.

Same as above but instead of the chocolate mix 2 tablespoons of very strong coffee to the sugar.

3)   White Icing.

Put together in a pan 3 tablespoons butter, 5 tablespoons cream. Bring it to a boil, take off fire and add, working gradually, two cups or more of granulated sugar. Teaspoon vanilla.

4)   Fudge Frosting.

1/2 lb. semi-sweet chocolate.
1/2 cup butter.

Combine and melt in double boiler. Beat until thick enough to spread.

5) Butter Frosting.

1/3 cup sweet butter.
1 cup confectioner's sugar.
flavoring.

Cream butter and sugar together. Add melted chocolate or strong coffee or both.

XX Petits Fours Meringués.

eggs   = 2 whites.
sugar   = 1/4 pound.
chocolate = 2 squares and a half.

Beat the eggs very stiff and fold very slowly the sugar and melted chocolate. (cold) (or use cocoa and more sugar.) Drop one teaspoon of the mixture at a time on a cooky sheet and bake in slow oven.

Petits fours meringués

XXI   Chestnut Cake.

This is a great delicacy in France and there are many
variations. I will only give two.

> 2 lbs. chestnuts.
> 1/4 lb. sugar.
> 1/4 lb. butter.
> 1/2 cup rum.

Peel the chestnuts and boil slowly in a covered pan for
about 30 minutes. Drain chestnuts and remove inner skin.
Put through food mill and while still hot (or in a double
boiler) mix thoroughly with it the sugar, butter and rum.
Work with a wooden spoon until you obtain a smooth paste.
Pour slowly into a buttered mold and chill overnight.

The next day unmold on a platter and serve with whipped cream
or cover with a chocolate icing.

> II   2 lbs. chestnuts.
> 1/2 lb. sugar.
> 2 cups heavy cream.

Cook chestnuts and put through food mill. Add sugar then
when cold the stiffly beaten cream. Pour in mold and chill
as in preceding recipe. Serve with or without chocolate
icing.

Gâteau aux marrons